# What I Had Was Singing

## THE STORY OF MARIAN ANDERSON

# What I Had Was Singing

## THE STORY OF MARIAN ANDERSON

Jeri Ferris

Carolrhoda Books, Inc./Minneapolis

*For my son Tom*
*Writer, editor, friend.*

My special thanks to Dr. H. Viscount Nelson, Jr., University of California, Los Angeles, for his invaluable help and advice; Rayner Mann, Los Angeles Unified School District, for her generous comments; and E. Marie Flenoury, musician, for her memories of Marian Anderson. Nancy Shawcross, Special Collections, Van Pelt Library, University of Pennsylvania, and Dr. Fritz Malval, Director of Archives, Hampton University, were most helpful in providing dates and documents.

*This book is available in two editions:*
Library binding by Carolrhoda Books, Inc.
Soft cover by First Avenue Editions
Carolrhoda Books, Inc. and First Avenue Editions
c/o The Lerner Group
241 First Avenue North
Minneapolis, Minnesota 55401

Library of Congress Cataloging-in-Publication Data

Ferris, Jeri.
   What I had was singing : the story of Marian Anderson / Jeri Ferris.
     p.  cm.—(Trailblazers)
   Includes bibliographical references and index.
   ISBN 0-87614-818-6 (lib. bdg.)
   ISBN 0-87614-634-5 (pbk.)
   1. Anderson, Marian, 1897–1993—Juvenile literature. 2. Contraltos—United States—Biography—Juvenile literature. 3. Afro-American singers—Biography—Juvenile literature. [1. Anderson, Marian, 1897–1993. 2. Singers. 3. Afro-Americans—Biography.] I. Title. II. Series: Trailblazers (Minneapolis, Minn.)
ML3930.A5F47  1994
782.1'092—dc20                        93-28502
[B]                                     CIP
                                          MN

Manufactured in the United States of America
2 3 4 5 6 7 – JR – 01 00 99 98 97 96

# Contents

# Introduction

"Nobody sees it," Marian Anderson said, "but it's there and you can feel it."

"It" was discrimination: being treated as less important and less valuable than a white person. It's what a black woman felt when she waited and waited for a trolley, only to have the white motorman pass her by. Or what a black man felt when he was turned down for a job he could do very well, and a white man was hired. It's what a black teenager felt when she went to a drugstore lunch counter with her money, but couldn't sit there even though there were empty seats. That's how it felt to be African American in the United States for most of Marian Anderson's life.

Marian Anderson felt this discrimination, but it didn't stop her or still her amazing voice. With that voice, and with determination to succeed, Marian Anderson helped smooth the path for Rosa Parks, Martin Luther King, Jr., and others—black and white—who work to make America a land of freedom and justice for all.

Children gather on the front steps of houses on a South Philadelphia
street, in the racially mixed neighborhood where Marian Anderson
was born.

# A Little Girl with a Big Voice

Some people know what they want to do from the very beginning. Marian Anderson did. She wanted to sing. From the very beginning, she said, music was more appealing than talk or toys.

Some people (but not many) remember being two years old. Marian Anderson did. She remembered singing at the top of her voice to the colorful flowers on the wallpaper in the living room, while she pounded away on a make-believe piano. (The piano was really just her little table, but she had a good imagination.)

And some people can do what they love best all their lives. Marian Anderson did.

Marian was born on February 27, 1897, in South Philadelphia, Pennsylvania, in the room that her parents had rented ever since they were married. When Marian was about two, they all moved in with her father's parents, and there her sister Alyce was born. They moved again, to a small house on Colorado Street, when her sister Ethel was born. In the warmth of that busy, crowded neighborhood of narrow brick row houses, the five of them thought they would live happily ever after.

Everybody in the mostly black neighborhood knew Marian. She skipped up the street to the market, she ran down the street to follow the cart horses, and sometimes she just stopped to chat with folks. She was always tall for her age, tall and slender like her father, with a wide smile full of joy and laughter. Even when Marian wasn't singing, people said her voice seemed full of music.

Marian's father, John, worked in the Reading Terminal Market, and he delivered coal and ice. He was also head usher at the large Union Baptist Church close to their home. Marian thought her father looked wonderfully handsome at church in his dark suit, as he made sure everyone found a seat and felt welcome.

Marian's mother, Anna, was so tiny she had to stand on tiptoe to tie her husband's necktie. Mrs. Anderson was quiet, but she always had the words to help her daughter, whether Marian had a small hurt on the outside from falling down, or a deep hurt on the inside because a white person had treated her rudely.

The Andersons didn't have much money, so for fun the family went out to the big green parks in Philadelphia.

Reading Terminal in the early 1900s. Marian's father, John Anderson, worked at the market inside the terminal.

Parks were free. And they went to the Barnum and Bailey Circus once a year. The circus wasn't free, but the grownups decided it was worth the money anyway.

On circus day, Mr. Anderson would buy something new for each girl to wear. (Once he bought a sailor hat for Marian, with a long ribbon to trail down her back.) Mrs. Anderson would pack a picnic basket, and they would all get up early for the long trolley ride to the circus grounds. (They had to allow time, too, in case the first motorman might not stop for black passengers.) That night they would return home late, hot and dusty and bubbling over with excited stories about the lumbering elephants, fierce tigers, and brave trapeze artists.

Sometimes, on rainy or cold evenings when they couldn't go out to sit on the front steps and visit with the neighbors, Marian and her family sang in their small front room. One good thing about singing, Marian often thought, was that she could sing while she did other things. And six-year-old Marian had lots of things to do to help her busy mother. She set the table, she swept the floor with her own little carpet sweeper, and she wiped Philadelphia's sooty coal dust off the furniture.

On summer days when the house turned into a sweltering brick oven, Marian might take her two little sisters out on the front steps to play. She had to watch carefully so they didn't run out into the street and fall under the heavy hooves of the cart horses, or, worst of all, fall in front of a trolley car. She might be singing in her head, but she could easily hear the clip-clop of horses' hooves and the clanking and buzzing of the trolleys.

When Marian started first grade, she had even more to do, and she learned the hard way that this included homework. One day her teacher called her to the front to give a book report. Marian twisted her fingers in the folds of her pink-checked dress and stammered some words about a book she hadn't read carefully. When her mother heard about it after school, she gave Marian some advice. "If it takes you half an hour to do your lessons and it takes someone else fifteen minutes," Mrs. Anderson said, "take the half hour and do them right." From then on, Marian took the time.

It didn't help that the classroom next door to Marian's was the music room. Every time children sang in that room, Marian stopped listening to her teacher and heard only the singing. Soon she knew every song, or at least she thought she did.

Finally the day arrived for Marian's class to go to the music room, and Marian thought she must be the happiest girl in the whole world. The moment the teacher began to play the first song, Marian took a deep breath, put her head back, and sang "Sleep, Polly, sleep" in a loud, clear voice.

The music teacher stopped playing. "Marian, what are you singing?" she asked. Look at the words on your music, the teacher insisted. Marian looked. She did not see "Sleep, Polly, sleep." She saw "Peacefully sleep," and her cheeks burned as she realized she had heard the words wrong through the wall. But whatever the words were, Marian was singing, and that made her the happiest girl in the world.

Before she was seven, Marian began singing in the Union Baptist children's choir. As soon as Alexander Robinson, the choir director, heard her sing, he knew she had a most unusual voice. So Mr. Robinson gave Marian and her friend Viola some music to take home to practice. It was a hymn called "Dear to the Heart of the Shepherd," which the girls were to sing in church.

The girls did so well that they were asked to sing again the next Sunday for even more people. Marian's big dark eyes glowed with delight at the congregation's applause, and her smile put dimples in her cheeks. The church was built to carry sounds well, and Marian filled the whole building with her rich young voice, all the way to the back corners of the balconies. In fact, Mr. Robinson had to remind her not to fill the building quite so loudly.

Although Marian was learning from her few trips downtown to go shopping that she was not always welcome outside her black community, she felt as secure as a princess *in* her community and in her church. She had her family and her music, and she sang for the people of her church several times a week.

Soon the people in Marian's church wanted others to hear her beautiful voice. On her way to the market one day, Marian saw a paper lying in the street. Something on the paper looked familiar. Marian picked it up and saw her own picture on it, with a notice saying "Come and hear the baby contralto, ten years old." Marian was so excited to see her picture on the advertisement that she rushed home with potatoes instead of the bread her mother had sent her to get. (Her mother sent her back.)

That same year, Marian's father bought a piano for the girls. He couldn't afford to pay for lessons too, and Marian didn't think she would ever learn to play well on her own. But when she was carrying a basket of laundry down the street for her mother, she heard the sound of a piano coming from a nearby row house. She set the basket down on the steps and peeped through the window. There she saw a woman with dark skin like hers, playing the piano beautifully.

Marian decided if that woman could learn to play, she could learn too. She found a picture of the keyboard that showed where middle C and the other notes were on the piano and what they looked like on a page of music.

This South Philadelphia market served black shoppers, but Marian found that outside her community, African Americans weren't always welcome.

After a lot of practice to get her fingers on the right notes at the right time, Marian finally learned to play so well that she could accompany herself while she sang. She especially loved the tricky key of D flat. That key was like velvet, Marian thought, perfect for her own low voice.

Marian's mother often said to her, "Remember, wherever you are and whatever you do, someone always sees you." Marian remembered how the woman she had seen playing the piano had helped her without even knowing it.

# 2

# Growing Up

When Marian was about twelve, her father died after a bad accident at work. The Andersons had no insurance or other help, and Mrs. Anderson could no longer afford the rent on their little house. Grandmother Anderson invited the sad and lonely family to live with her on Fitzwater Street. Marian's aunt and two daughters, Queenie and Grace Anderson, also lived with Grandmother and Grandfather Anderson. That made five Anderson girls, and that made plenty of work, so Marian didn't have time (or room) to be lonely.

Grandmother Anderson was a tall, strong woman who was part American Indian and made sure everyone knew it. She also made sure everyone in the house kept busy. Grandfather Anderson, now the only man in a family of nine, was quiet and hardworking. He was very religious, but he did not go to the Union Baptist Church. Grandfather was Jewish, and from him Marian learned the meaning of Passover and other Jewish traditions.

The Union Baptist Church as it looks today. A plaque outside tells passersby that Marian Anderson sang here.

Even after her father died, Marian continued to go to the Union Baptist Church each Sunday. Marian loved Sundays. Sundays meant singing and church and friends at church and friends over for dinner. She went to parties, spelling bees, and musical events at church all during the week, too. In her warm circle of friends, Marian was one of the tallest and prettiest of the girls. Her smile, her friend Marie said, was "like the sun coming up."

Marian was invited to join the adult choir at church when she was only thirteen, and she continued to sing with the children in the junior choir, too. Her voice was just naturally so splendid and her range so wide that she could sing not only her own low alto part, but also the tenor (even lower) and the soprano (higher) parts.

The Union Baptist Church choir was known for its beautiful music. Now that Marian was in the adult choir, she traveled with them when the choir performed for other churches and in other cities. Of course it was expensive for the entire choir to travel, so often only a quartet (four singers) or a duet (two singers) would travel. Marian was always one of the singers, and if only one could be sent, Marian was the one.

By this time, singing before large audiences was as natural and necessary to Marian as breathing. She knew her singing gave pleasure to those who heard it, and deep in her heart what she wanted most in all the world was to study and to make music. (Marian had taken music classes, but she had never studied *singing*. She just sang.)

But Marian also knew she had to be practical. When she entered William Penn High School, she decided that the right thing was to take classes to learn to be a secretary. Then, as soon as she finished high school, she could go straight to work and help her mother support the family.

Marian bravely started in on typing, shorthand, and bookkeeping. Alas, her heart was not in these studies. She practiced and practiced the wiggly lines and loops and hooks that are shorthand, but when the teacher began dictating a letter to the class, Marian fell hopelessly behind. She was still making the lines and loops for "Dear Sir," when the teacher (and the rest of the class) was finished with the whole first sentence. Bookkeeping was even worse. Her heart sank when she looked at all those rows of numbers, and she felt that she was in very deep water indeed.

By 1918 Marian was appearing in concert not just in Philadelphia's black churches and colleges, but also at larger concert halls, including the Philadelphia Academy of Music.

Marian struggled on with her business classes, determined to get a secretarial job and *maybe* even to pay for music lessons for herself someday. The only bright spot in her week was music class. The music teacher recognized Marian's talent for singing and gave her solos in school assemblies as often as possible.

After singing at an assembly one day, Marian was called to the principal's office. She couldn't think of anything she'd done wrong, but her heart pounded as she hurried down the hall. When she got to the office, the principal introduced her to Dr. Rohrer, who had just heard her sing. Pointing to Marian, Dr. Rohrer said, "I don't understand why this girl is taking shorthand and typewriting. She should have a straight college preparatory course and do as much as possible in music."

No sooner said than done. Marian transferred to South Philadelphia High School, where the principal, Dr. Lucy Wilson, was very interested in Marian's musical ability. Dr. Wilson brought well-known professional performers to her high school and made sure Marian had many opportunities to sing in public.

During these high school years, Marian sang in front of audiences almost every day. There was always an event or two taking place in the black churches of Philadelphia, and sometimes Marian was asked to sing at three different churches in one evening. Soon she was invited to sing at black colleges and churches outside the city, too. Marian missed many days of school because of her singing engagements, but her teachers understood and let her work her way through high school slowly.

Dr. Lucy Wilson, principal, South Philadelphia High School, in 1915

Now Marian was helping to pay the family bills without the torture of bookkeeping and shorthand. She was earning money doing the thing she loved most—and she was beginning to hope that music and singing could actually be her career.

Marian didn't know of many professional singers in her African-American community, but she did know about the famous black tenor, Roland Hayes. His singing was "the most beautiful and inspiring" Marian had ever heard. Mr. Hayes was successful in the white world of classical music. He was a generous, handsome, gracious person. And he was Marian's hero.

Roland Hayes was one of the first black American singers to achieve international success.

Mr. Hayes was invited every year for a special concert at Marian's church. He always included a number of songs in Italian, German, and French on his concert program. Some in the audience complained that they couldn't understand what he was singing, but, they said, "If our Marian were on the program, we would understand what *she* was singing about." And so Marian was permitted to sing on the same program as Roland Hayes.

Marian was so excited and nervous she couldn't sleep the night before the concert, but she sang with all her natural richness and grace. Mr. Hayes was stunned by her voice. He immediately made arrangements for Marian to take voice lessons with his own teacher, Mr.

Arthur Hubbard in Boston. Then Mr. Hayes called on Grandmother Anderson to tell her of this wonderful opportunity for Marian.

Grandmother Anderson was not impressed. She did not agree that Marian needed special lessons. Mr. Hayes tried his best to sway her, but Grandmother Anderson's mind was made up. Marian would not go to Boston.

Marian's mother could not oppose her mother-in-law. Marian would not dream of opposing Grandmother Anderson either, but she was greatly disappointed. Marian's chance to study singing had passed, but she tried hard not to regret it. She tried to put it out of her mind as something that was not meant to be. She tried to believe, as her mother did, that something better would come along for her.

# 3

# A Beginning

Another chance came along while Marian was still in high school. Her first voice teacher, Mary S. Patterson, was a black woman who lived in the neighborhood. Mrs. Patterson charged one dollar a lesson, which Marian had a hard time paying, so the teacher kindly said she would provide lessons free of charge.

Before beginning the first lesson, Mrs. Patterson asked Marian how she produced a note. Marian looked at her teacher blankly. As far as she knew, she simply opened her mouth and there it was. A high C note, a low D, whatever she needed.

This was not good enough for Mrs. Patterson, who immediately began teaching Marian to direct her voice toward a corner of the ceiling. Project your voice, she said, throw it toward that faraway corner. Think, she said, think and control your voice. At first it was difficult for

Marian to stop and think about *how* she sang, instead of just singing. But she gladly worked and finally was able to project an entire song.

The more Marian sang, and the more she heard professional singers, the more she wanted to be able to attend a music school. While she was studying with Mrs. Patterson, she decided to inquire at a music school in Philadelphia. Marian wasn't sure whether or not she would be able to afford classes at the school, but she could hardly wait to find out. Even if it was very expensive, she thought, something could surely be worked out.

On the day for new students to sign up, Marian arrived at the music school early. She took her place in the enrollment line and listened as the people in front of her asked their questions of the young white woman at the window. Marian was just thinking how pretty the young woman was, and how lucky she was to work in a place filled with the joy and beauty of music, when her turn came at the window.

To Marian's surprise, the pretty young woman looked right past her at the next person in line. Marian was so startled that she couldn't think what to do, or what was wrong. Wasn't she old enough to attend? Marian stood in shocked silence while every single other person was waited on. Finally, there was no one left but Marian.

"What do *you* want?" the girl said.

Marian explained politely that she wanted an application to the school.

"We don't take colored," the girl said with a toss of her blond curls.

Marian was so stunned she couldn't speak. She stared with wide eyes at the girl, and the thought that such words could come from another young person, and one surrounded by music at that, overwhelmed her. What was worse, the girl seemed to *like* saying it. Marian shuddered, feeling as if an icy hand had closed around her heart. She turned away from the window without protesting and left the music school.

Of course Marian knew there were places where she and her family and other black people could not go (ordinary places such as hotels, restaurants, a swimming pool). She knew there were people who did not want to associate with her. She had stood in stores with her money ready, waiting and waiting, while white people were helped first. But never, never, had she been refused a thing she really wanted because of the color of her skin.

As she walked slowly down the sidewalk, Marian wondered if other music schools would reject her too. The bright and shining excitement she had felt earlier was gone, and she couldn't stop shaking. She decided that she must put the idea of music school out of her mind completely, because the thought of another such rejection was unbearable.

At home Marian went straight to the kitchen and sank into a chair. Her mother left the washing in the sink and sat at the table with Marian, shaking her head as she listened. There was nothing she could do to change what had happened, but she did have words of encouragement. "A way will be found," Mrs. Anderson said, squeezing Marian's hands firmly.

A way *was* found. At Mrs. Patterson's suggestion, Marian moved on to a new and more challenging voice teacher, Agnes Reifsnyder. Miss Reifsnyder was a contralto, so she was well prepared to work with Marian's own low contralto voice. She concentrated on Marian's breathing techniques, on her low tones, and introduced her to the songs of Brahms. Johannes Brahms, a nineteenth-century German composer, wrote music of such tenderness and beauty that his songs are part of every classical singer's program. His songs were exactly what Marian wanted.

Marian learned so quickly that she was ready to move on to a third voice teacher while still in high school. Dr. Wilson helped arrange for Marian to sing for Giuseppe Boghetti. Mr. Boghetti was a famous, demanding, dynamic, and difficult voice teacher. He greeted Marian by saying that he was only doing this as a favor. Furthermore, he said severely, he had no time or space for another student.

With this discouraging news, Marian's audition began. She sang the spiritual "Deep River," her rich voice floating to the far corners of the room, her eyes avoiding the stern Mr. Boghetti. Even when the song was over, and the tones still vibrated, she could not look at the famous man.

For a moment no one moved. Finally Mr. Boghetti cleared his throat. "I will make room for you right away," he said, "and I will need only two years with you. After that, you will be able to go anywhere and sing for anybody."

Her new teacher immediately discovered some flaws. Marian had trouble with breathing techniques. In the heat of a song, she just breathed and sang, and if she had enough breath for the song, she forgot about technique. She had to learn to sing up and down the scale without any change in quality of tone from the highest note to the lowest note. She also needed to work on her pianissimo, a very soft and quiet singing voice.

And she needed to decide what kind of singer she would become. When Marian sang spirituals, she sang from her own rich experience and culture. Spirituals were her own music. They were part of every program she ever sang. She was a singer of spirituals. But the majesty, tenderness, and power of classical music also spoke to Marian's heart.

Giuseppe Boghetti was a demanding and expensive voice teacher. Marian's church raised $600 for her lessons with Mr. Boghetti.

With Mr. Boghetti, Marian worked toward her goal of becoming a great classical singer. Mr. Boghetti taught her the songs of Robert Schumann, Sergei Rachmaninoff, and Franz Schubert, in addition to more songs by Brahms. He also taught her French and English songs and Italian arias, or elaborate solo songs.

Marian realized that she needed to learn several languages in order to sing a full classical concert program correctly. In high school she studied French, and with Mr. Boghetti she studied Italian. But she didn't know anyone who could teach her German. So, when she sang Schubert and Brahms (who both wrote in German), she did it phonetically, without understanding what she was saying. That didn't work. Still, she and Mr. Boghetti did what they could.

Marian had only a half-hour lesson each week, but if the next student was late, Mr. Boghetti let her continue. Or, if the next student didn't mind, Marian listened in on that lesson too.

It was difficult for Marian to practice properly for her lessons. She would not sing out loud at home for fear of disturbing the neighbors, so she took the music to bed with her and said the words over and over, singing the notes in her head. The day of her lesson she would take her music to school and study it when she should have been studying her classwork. Marian knew Mr. Boghetti could be a terrifying teacher. She had seen students leave in tears and heard him say if they did not study he did not want them. She studied.

Even with all that studying, Marian found time for fun.

At a party after one of her concerts, Marian met Orpheus Fisher, nicknamed King. King was a young black architecture student who took quite a liking to Marian. In fact, it wasn't long before he asked her to marry him. Marian liked King, but her music came first. She wasn't ready to get serious. So Marian sang and went to high school, while King studied architecture and waited for Marian to agree to his proposal.

While she was still in high school, Marian first met Jim Crow. "Jim Crow" was not a person—it was another name for segregation, the way that whites kept black people away from white people. Jim Crow was the law in the southern United States.

Marian and her mother went together on Marian's first long trip south to give a concert. The train ride from Philadelphia to Washington, D.C., was a pleasure. Then in Washington, a traditionally southern city, they had to change trains. There, the porter put their bags in a Jim Crow car—for blacks only. When Marian followed him up the metal steps, she could hardly believe what she saw: a filthy train car, with bad lighting, dirty windows, and no ventilation. The car was just behind the engine, so if she opened the window for air, the smoke and ashes from the engine blew into her face and eyes. Marian and her mother sat up all night in that dirty Jim Crow car, and Marian thought the night would never end.

In Savannah, Georgia, they were greeted kindly and had a most pleasant visit and concert. But they had to return to Washington, D.C., in that same Jim Crow train car.

In the early 1920s, when Marian was making her first concert tours of the south, she encountered Jim Crow waiting rooms, like this one at the train depot in Jacksonville, Florida.

The thought of it filled Marian's heart with dread. When they got to the train station, Marian steeled herself. She straightened her shoulders and kept her face calm, but inside she was shaking with shame and humiliation. She could hardly bear to look at her mother's face, for there she saw the same shame. Marian could not understand how such things could be.

# 4

# Defeat, and Recovery

Marian graduated from high school in June 1921. She had missed many semesters, but she always made up the work and she proudly received her diploma. Now, without classes and homework, she could sing any time, anywhere. William (Billy) King, a prominent accompanist for visiting artists including Roland Hayes, became her regular accompanist. Billy scheduled their concerts, which were given in black colleges, black churches, black professional theaters, and occasionally in larger halls such as the Philadelphia Academy of Music. At the same time, Marian's fee for a concert rose until it passed fifty dollars and went on up to one hundred dollars.

In 1923, when she was twenty-six, Marian became the first black person to win the Philadelphia Philharmonic Society's singing contest. Her achievement was widely reported in the newspapers, and reviews of her concerts began to appear in papers other than those published only for the African-American community. For the first time, white people, or "people not of my group," as Marian called them, took notice of her work. She began to hope that she could be successful before large audiences of white concertgoers too.

Not long after the philharmonic contest, Marian made a fateful decision. She and Mr. Boghetti scheduled an April 1924 concert in New York's grand Town Hall to prove her ability as a professional classical singer. Marian was sure she would be well received by white audiences now, and the Town Hall performance would be the first in her successful career before all classical music lovers. She paid all the expenses to rent the hall, rent the piano, and print the program. And she agreed to take no money for her performance—the fame would be enough.

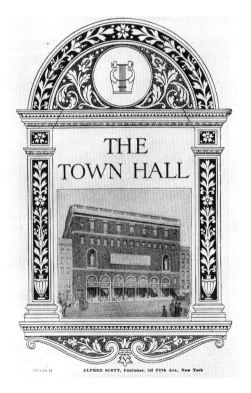

Marian's concert at New York City's Town Hall in April 1924 was to be a test of her abilities as a professional classical singer.

In addition to her program of English, Russian, and Italian music, Marian added four new songs by Brahms, to be sung in German. She could hardly wait to sing these lovely songs in a great hall, as she had heard Roland Hayes do with such skill and understanding. Unfortunately, Marian had to memorize the songs syllable by syllable because, unlike Mr. Hayes, she still didn't know German well enough to understand the words she sang.

The hall was rented, the tickets were on sale, and finally the day of Marian's New York City concert arrived. Marian got to New York early in the afternoon. She tried to rest at the Harlem YWCA, but she was too excited to sit still. She kept smiling inside and outside, thinking of all the people who would hear her that evening.

Billy King arrived, they rehearsed together, and they waited for the hour of the concert. The young man who had organized the concert came backstage to assure Marian that there would be a full house, and again Marian's heart soared with happiness and excitement.

The time to go onstage came. Marian was not called. Then 8:45 came and went. Finally at nine o'clock, she was told to go onstage.

Marian walked out confidently and looked over the great hall. To her horror, she saw only a few people scattered here and there in the entire place. Marian's heart sank to her shoes, and she felt her enthusiasm escape like air from a balloon. She felt quite alone.

Marian took a deep breath, bowed and smiled as usual, and tried to look confident. But she was almost overwhelmed with misery. She nodded to Billy, at the far end of the stage, and the program began. When she came to the songs by Brahms, Marian sang the German she had so carefully practiced, but she knew something was not right. The program dragged on to its conclusion. As Billy King closed his music, the faint clapping from here and there in the huge hall seemed worse, somehow, than no clapping at all. Marian bowed automatically and left the stage. Her long-awaited debut was over.

In the morning, the reviews were not good. Marian's German songs in particular were pointed out as bad examples of singing in a language that one did not know.

Marian was devastated with shame and embarrassment. She realized, too late, that she had not been ready for a New York debut. She returned to Philadelphia and tried to blot out the pain of the evening. Closed up in her room, Marian felt totally defeated for the first time in her life. Worst of all, she knew she deserved those reviews.

"That part of my life is finished," she told herself.

Her dream of becoming a famous singer had been just a dream. Now, Marian believed, her dream was ended. Only two things kept Marian from utter despair: her mother's wise counsel and support; and their own little house, bought with a down payment of six hundred dollars from Marian's savings.

The house was Marian's pride and joy. There were two bedrooms for four people, which worked out nicely for Marian, her mother, and her two sisters. There were new hardwood floors, a large kitchen, and for the first time, her own music studio. But now, like Marian, the house was gloomy and silent.

With her earnings from singing, Marian bought this row house in South Philadelphia in the 1920s.

During those months of discouragement, Marian looked for another career. Medicine was the only other career she could imagine, but as she thought more and more, the conviction returned that "nothing in life, not even medicine, could be so important as music." Still, Marian avoided singing. She retreated to the small studio that had been built out of the upstairs bathroom in their little house. There she thought and brooded. Her singing had always helped support the family, and as the oldest daughter, she felt all the more responsible. Even though the memory of her failure weighed heavily on her spirit, responsibility for her family weighed even more.

Marian's pain and disappointment over the concert gradually eased as she talked about it with her mother. "I had wanted so very much to sing well enough to please everybody," Marian said, over and over.

"Listen, my child," her mother said gently. "Whatever you do in this world, no matter how good it is, you will never be able to please everybody. All you can strive for is to do the best it is humanly possible for you to do."

Anna Anderson, Marian's mother. Mrs. Anderson's words, "Do not let hate or fear restrict you from being a big person," helped Marian through difficult times.

As time passed, Marian began to practice quietly. She sang a little, then more and more frequently as joy returned. Finally she went back to Mr. Boghetti and to concert touring with Billy King. Soon Marian had a busy schedule filled with successes. She was happy again, happy to be singing and happy to be helping her mother pay the family's bills.

Mrs. Anderson had worked without stopping since Marian's father died. For a long time, she had taken in laundry and had cleaned other people's houses. Recently she had taken a cleaning job at Wanamaker's Department Store. Marian saw how desperately hard her mother worked, and her heart hurt for her. Mrs. Anderson's income was helpful to the family, but Marian began to look for a way to get along without it.

One day her mother came home feeling too sick to eat dinner. The doctor came, told her she must stay in bed, and left some medicine.

Early the next morning, Mrs. Anderson was up getting ready for work. She looked absolutely terrible but insisted she must go. Marian and her sisters insisted that she must not go and put her in bed. During the days her mother was sick, Marian went over their finances again and came to a decision. She alone could and would provide for her family's needs.

She picked up the telephone and called Wanamaker's. She was so excited she could hardly sit still but managed to stay calm while she politely told the supervisor that Mrs. Anderson would not be working there anymore. When Marian hung up, she felt as if she would burst with happiness before she could run up to her mother's room.

As she sat on the edge of her mother's small, neat bed and looked into her mother's tired eyes, Marian knew her decision was right. Quietly, simply, she told her mother she wouldn't have to work anymore.

It was one of the happiest moments of Marian's life.

In the summer of 1925, Marian entered a major singing contest in New York City with a guest appearance with the New York Philharmonic Orchestra as first prize. She went to Mr. Boghetti several times a week to rehearse her contest pieces, a long aria and two shorter songs in case the judges asked to hear more. Her aria was the dramatic and emotional "O mio Fernando" from Gaetano Donizetti's opera *La Favorita.*

On the big day, Marian took the train to New York and went with Mr. Boghetti to Aeolian Hall for the competition. She joined three hundred eager contestants milling about the hot, stuffy auditorium. Marian knew the competition would be difficult. She felt tense and excited and hot, but not afraid.

She thought about the rule the judges had made: if they sounded a clicker, the singer was to stop immediately and leave the stage. She knew the judges had made this rule because they had to hear over one hundred contestants each day, in stifling heat. But Mr. Boghetti told her that, clicker or not, she must continue singing to the end of the aria.

Marian's turn came toward the end of the first day. She had already heard at least six other singers begin "O mio Fernando," only to be stopped by the dreadful clicker. She weighed Mr. Boghetti's advice against the judges' rule, and as she walked onto the stage, Marian decided that she must obey the rule. If she heard the clicker, she would stop.

Marian began calmly, richly, but with a part of her listening for "the voice of doom." It didn't come.

She soared on through the entire aria. Then one of the judges called from the balcony, "Does 44A have another song?" Marian sang once more and left the stage.

Marian returned to Philadelphia not knowing what the judges thought. She decided to continue the swimming lessons she had already started to escape the extreme heat. So every day she went faithfully to the pool at the South Philadelphia YWCA, and every day she stood fearfully in the shallow end. ("I am like a stone in the water," she said.) She didn't learn to swim. She did get a severe ear infection—just when she needed to be at her best in case the judges called her back.

The good news came a few days later. She had been selected one of sixteen semifinalists and was to return to New York. The bad news was that the pain in Marian's ear made it difficult for her to move her jaw and project her voice fully.

It was terribly hot and muggy in Aeolian Hall on the day of the semifinals. Marian sang her aria and her two extra songs in a haze of pain, barely able to hear her own voice. No one said anything to her about how well or how poorly she had done, and her only thought was to get home to Philadelphia as fast as possible. She was beginning to worry that she might lose her hearing and never sing again anyway.

Mr. Boghetti insisted they stop at his studio in New York on the way to the train, just in case there was any word from the judges. As Marian huddled in a chair, the phone rang, and a minute later Mr. Boghetti shouted, "We have won! There will be no finals!"

Marian stood up to go to the door. Mr. Boghetti, who was so excited he was jumping around the room, cried, "Where are you going?"

"Home," Marian answered. She knew Mr. Boghetti was disappointed, but her ear hurt so much that she couldn't think of anything else.

She took the seven o'clock train back to Philadelphia. Home at last, Marian set down her music and told her mother she was going to see the family doctor. Fortunately the doctor lived just down the street. By the time he was finished, and had assured her that she would not become deaf, Marian felt better in every way.

Now she could get excited. The next day the Philadelphia newspapers told about Marian's prize. She would make a guest appearance with the New York Philharmonic Orchestra at Lewisohn Stadium on August 26, 1925.

Marian practiced until she was sure she would not fail. She had had one disaster in New York, and she never wanted another one. When she took her place onstage that August night, she looked out on a sea of faces, black and white. Her family and Mr. Boghetti were there in front, and so was the still-hopeful King Fisher. It was a beautiful, balmy evening, and the open-air stadium with its rows of long, circular concrete steps was packed. Marian felt shaky with excitement, but not frightened. When the audience applauded even before she sang, she was filled with a wonderful warmth.

She sang her prizewinning solo, "O mio Fernando," several spirituals, and finally several joyous encores, all with the utmost confidence and ease. Not only the audience, but also the orchestra, applauded so loudly and with such appreciation that Marian felt as if the whole starry sky could not contain her happiness. When she finally left the stage, with a bouquet of red roses in her arms, the pain of the Town Hall fiasco was behind her for good.

Now, she felt sure, she would be accepted on any stage as a serious classical singer. But a year after her prize-winning concert, Marian's high hopes began to fade. Her audiences were larger and her fees were higher, but her performances were in the same places they had always been. She decided unhappily that her career was at a standstill.

Perhaps a new voice teacher would help? Marian considered studying with Frank La Forge, a well-known voice teacher with many contacts in the musical world. Leaving Mr. Boghetti was difficult to think about, but after several sleepless nights, Marian finally concluded that she must at least try the experience of another teacher.

Frank La Forge taught Marian at his New York City studio. Marian was up before sunrise so she could be in New York by 9 o'clock.

Marian worked with Mr. La Forge for more than a year and made great progress. She even tried singing in German again.

But one evening in a small recital, Marian sang in German, and the performer's nightmare happened—she forgot some of the words. She had to make up words in a language she didn't know. Marian was so embarrassed she could hardly stand it, and although she was seldom ever nervous, this experience gave her chills. It kept haunting her, and the fear that it would happen again forced her to decide that she must learn to speak German fluently, immediately, or never sing in German again.

# 5

# Europe

The evening of the forgotten words finally sent Marian to Europe. The expense was frightening, but after going over the family budget one more time, Marian decided she must make the investment. She had to learn German and she had to move her career forward. Perhaps, she thought, not only the European training but also the European *experience* would help her career. After all, Roland Hayes had studied in Europe. Marian's decision was confirmed when she was given a small scholarship by the National Association of Negro Musicians.

Once she decided to go, Marian was so busy getting ready that she hardly had time to worry about money. She had to choose the correct clothes to take and find a trunk to hold them. She had to get maps, phone numbers, addresses, and introductions to the right people. And she had to buy a new music case to hold all the music she wanted to study on her trip.

Marian sailed from New York Harbor on a summer day in 1927. She stood at the crowded deck waving goodbye to her family and friends until the shore disappeared from view, and the ship *Ile de France* began steaming its way across the Atlantic. Then she went straight to her tiny second-class cabin and unpacked. There were many other Americans on board, but Marian was the only black American. She was left alone (and lonely) for the whole two-week voyage.

Finally the ship arrived at the docks in Southampton, England, and Marian went to Paddington Station in London by train. There she found a pay phone and called Roger Quilter, the man who was to make arrangements for Marian's stay in London. The phone rang and rang until a man answered.

"This is Marian Anderson," Marian said. "I have just arrived."

"Who?" said the man.

Marian took a deep breath and repeated her name slowly. The man had never heard of her. This was indeed a bad beginning, Marian thought. It turned out that the man was Mr. Quilter's butler, and poor Mr. Quilter was in the hospital. The butler didn't know a thing about Marian or what to do with her. Marian thanked him and hung up.

She told herself to stay calm and think. She had two coats over one arm, her overnight bag and purse on the other arm, her music case next to the telephone, and her trunk outside the booth. It was already dark out. Then she remembered John Payne, a black actor who had visited the Andersons' home in South Philadelphia years before. He lived in London, and he had told Marian to look him up if she ever came to England. This seemed to be the right moment.

Mr. Payne answered the phone. To Marian's delight, he invited her to come right over and stay with his family. Marian hurried to catch a taxi to 17 Regents Park Road. It was almost midnight when she arrived, but Mr. Payne was waiting at the door to greet her. He was so pleased to see her, and so curious about her career, that they sat up and talked until two in the morning.

When Marian picked up her things to go to the guest room, she couldn't find her music case. It wasn't there, anywhere. Mr. Payne assured her that they would find it in the morning and wished her a good night. But Marian did not have a good night. She couldn't sleep at all. She went over and over when she last had her music case and tried to imagine what she would do if it could not be found. It held everything she needed; in addition to her music, books, and notes, it contained every dollar she had.

The next day, Marian and the Paynes went to Paddington Station. And there, in Lost Property, was Marian's case with every dollar safe inside. It had been found in the phone booth right where she had left it. Marian gratefully left a generous tip and, with a deep sigh of relief, got ready to enjoy her stay.

After a few days in London, Marian repacked her bags and set off on the train for Sussex, where she would study German songs with the best teacher in England. As the train puffed over gently rolling green hills, Marian settled into a comfortable seat in a spacious, clean car. She remembered the shaming and filthy Jim Crow train cars she was put into when she traveled south in her own

country, and for a moment the harsh knot of tension returned. But it lasted only a moment. To Marian's joy
and relief, she was treated with the same kindness as
any other passenger. No one frowned at her. No one
got up and moved away from her. No one seemed to
care that her skin was darker than theirs. On this train,
Marian felt free.

Marian called on her teacher, Master Raimund von Zur
Mühlen, as soon as she arrived. Master, as he was called, was quite old and sat in a large chair at the end of
his long music room. He had a red rug across his knees
and a cane that he pounded on the floor when he wanted
anyone's attention. Marian concentrated on breathing
slowly and deeply, but she felt a twinge of fear in Master's
presence. He told her to sing something in German.
When she finished, he said, "Come here."

All the way down that long room, Marian dreaded what
Master would say. When she finally reached his chair,
he asked bluntly if she knew what she was singing.

"Not word for word...," she confessed. "I know what
it's about, but I don't know it word for word."

"That's not enough," Master said sternly.

Marian tried again. This time she sang the spiritual
"My Lord, What a Morning" in English, confidently and
proudly. Too proudly, it seemed, because Master immediately began striking the floor with his cane. "You're
singing like a queen," he growled, "and I have not
crowned you yet."

Gruff as he was, Marian thought there was kindness
in him, and they talked for a little while before she left.

He sent a Schubert song with her for homework. With some help, she translated the words so she would understand the song and practiced for her first lesson.

Again Master pounded his cane on the floor, frequently stopping Marian in midphrase, but by the end of the lesson, Marian felt she was really making progress. Alas, her first lesson with Master was her last. He became very ill. Although Marian stayed in Sussex for several weeks, waiting hopefully and practicing the Schubert, Master gave up teaching completely.

It was a dreadful disappointment. Marian had come to England to study German songs with Master and had had one lesson. Sadly, she returned to London.

Marian sang frequently in the autumn of 1928 in London. She sang for John Payne, for Roger Quilter, who was now out of the hospital, and for other music lovers. She gained experience and confidence, but all too soon her time in England was up.

After an uneventful voyage, Marian was back in Philadelphia, hugging her mother and sisters. She walked through each room of their little house. She walked up and down the street greeting her neighbors. And then she sat down to look at her mail and her concert schedule for the winter season. There were only seventeen concerts for five months, fewer than four per month, and all were in the same churches, the same colleges, the same local halls. Marian could hardly believe it. She read the schedule again, and her joy at being home drained away. All the time and money she had just spent on her stay in England seemed to be for nothing.

Marian was not home long before she decided that she must return to Europe, this time to Germany. She had tried to study German with the best teacher in England, and that had not worked. So again, in spring 1930, Marian and her music case and her trunk left New York Harbor, this time on a German ship bound for Germany. Two weeks later she completed her trip by train to Berlin.

Marian on board ship, crossing the Atlantic to Germany. When Marian asked her mother what she could bring her from Europe, Mrs. Anderson replied that she only wanted God to hold Marian "in the hollow of His hand."

Marian found a room at the home of Herr and Frau von Edburg, who did not speak a single word of English. This forced Marian to learn German quickly. With a German dictionary and reading book, and with Herr von Edburg as her teacher, she made rapid progress.

Her objective in Berlin was to study German lieder, love poems set to music. At the same time, she would be learning the language. Marian immediately began singing lessons with Herr Michael Raucheisen to build on her improving German language skills. Soon Marian felt that she was beginning to understand the meaning of her songs.

With the help of teachers in Germany, Marian finally began to understand German *lieder.* Each little *lied* (love poem) told a story of innocence, yearning, and heartbreak.

One day in Raucheisen's studio, two strangers entered as Marian was singing. They sat quietly until she finished. Rulle Rasmussen, a concert manager from Norway, and Kosti Vehanen, a pianist from Finland, were traveling through Europe looking for new talent. When they heard Marian, they knew they had found it. Mr.

Rasmussen asked Marian to come to Norway for a series of concerts with Mr. Vehanen as her accompanist.

Marian was flattered and delighted with the prospect of touring Scandinavia, but first she had a major concert to perform in Berlin. She was determined that this European trip, unlike her stay in London, would result in a great career advance. She had already reserved the Bachsaal Concert Hall in Berlin at a cost of five hundred dollars, which was most of her money. Marian intended to prove herself by singing lieder before German concertgoers.

On the night of the concert at the Bachsaal, Herr Raucheisen, who was also her accompanist, was so nervous that Marian had to have confidence for two people. When she looked at Herr Raucheisen, shaking and muttering to himself, with his mother trying to reassure him, she almost had to laugh. Here she was, giving her first major concert in Germany, before people who probably knew by heart the songs she would sing in their language, and her *teacher* was falling apart.

Marian managed to stay reasonably confident, and she and Herr Raucheisen walked onstage. The hall was full. Marian bowed, closed her eyes so that she saw only within herself, and began to sing. She remained calm, even though the audience seemed cold and unresponsive at first. By the time Marian finished her third song, there was warm applause and she began to feel a wonderful connection with her listeners. On and on she sang, carrying her audience with her and ending with a bow of thanks to loud applause.

Backstage, Herr Raucheisen said with relief, "Didn't I tell you it was going to be fine?" Marian just smiled and decided not to remind him of his nervousness. Besides, she was busy signing autographs and trying to understand what people were saying to her. It seemed to be all complimentary, as far as she could tell, and so were the reviews in the German papers.

Soon after the Bachsaal concert, Marian received a schedule of concerts from Mr. Rasmussen in Norway. She was to sing six times in Norway and Finland if all went well. Marian carefully selected evening dresses for concerts, and warm clothes for sight-seeing, and took the train to Oslo.

At their first rehearsal, her accompanist, Kosti Vehanen, was stunned by her voice. It was even more glorious than he had remembered. Kosti felt the whole room begin to vibrate as Marian sang her first note. Her voice seemed to swell with power, as a flower opens its petals, and it seemed to Kosti that the sound came from the earth itself. Three octaves, he marveled, low C to middle C to high C without effort and without a break in her tone.

Marian's six concerts quickly sold out, and more were added. As more and more people heard her, they began writing to her, requesting favorite songs. People telephoned her and stopped her on the street. They brought flowers and even music that they wanted her to sing for them in concert.

Everywhere, Marian was amazed by the warmth of the people. Many Scandinavians spoke English, and Marian learned a little Finnish from Kosti. Kosti was also fluent in German, so he was of great help with her German lieder. And he knew French, Italian, and English. Kosti was, in fact, as proficient in five languages as he was at the piano. He was the perfect accompanist for Marian.

Marian found the Scandinavians quite curious about her skin color, as well as her voice. This open-hearted curiosity did not bother Marian in the slightest. It was, she said, "a kind of wonder." One newspaper said she was the color of "café au lait" (coffee with milk). After a concert for which she wore one of her favorite blue gowns, a newspaper described her as "dressed in electric-blue satin and looking very much like a chocolate bar." Marian laughed when she heard that and wondered if she could ever wear her favorite dress again without laughing onstage.

In Scandinavia, as in England, Marian found that people accepted her as herself and did not seem influenced by her "outward difference." She could eat in the same dining room as anyone else. She could have a pleasant room in a pleasant hotel. She could even have her laundry done, just as anyone else could. The weight of prejudice was gone, and she felt free and light.

Marian began expressing her feelings in song with greater freedom. She was buoyed up by the enthusiasm of her audiences, by applause that went on and on. This response brought her greater confidence than she had felt before, and this, far more than the small fees she earned, was the great value of her trip. She dared to hope again that her dream of becoming a world-recognized artist could come true.

Marian in Sweden in the early 1930s. Marian took many horse-drawn sleigh rides in Scandinavia and grew to love the silence of the thick forests bent down with snow.

Her time in Europe was over all too soon, and Marian returned home, expecting *this* time to find a much improved concert schedule. She found a schedule that was the same as before: the same churches, the same schools, the same number of performances.

Marian wasn't sure exactly what was needed to move her career forward, but she wasn't finding it at home. In 1933 Marian returned to Europe. This time she stayed for two years.

# 6

# A Voice Heard Once in a Hundred Years

Marian hadn't actually intended to remain in Europe for two years, but as her popularity grew, so did her concert schedule. In just one year, she sang over one hundred concerts, to full houses, all over Scandinavia.

From her triumphs in Scandinavia, Marian went to London, and then to Paris in the early summer of 1935. Her first concert in Paris was sparsely attended, but Marian's spirits were high, and the confidence she had gained the past year shone through her music. She sang with ease in Italian, German, and English, and even one song in French.

The audience of a few hundred Parisians received Marian warmly, and the reviews were positive. The Paris concert manager, Mr. Fritz Horowitz, scheduled a second concert. This one was almost sold out, and Mr. Horowitz suggested a third performance for the middle of June.

Marian hesitated. She was alone in Paris. She thought of all kinds of excuses for not singing a third program and decided that she definitely could not do it. "Out of the question," she said firmly. Fortunately Mr. Horowitz won.

The third concert, on a lovely evening in the middle of June 1935, was completely sold out, and the next day's reviews pronounced Marian a "tremendous success." Of course Marian had been singing long enough to know that one concert wouldn't change her career. But this one did.

By chance, Sol Hurok, a famous and powerful American theatrical agent for artists such as Anna Pavlova and Benny Goodman, was vacationing in Paris. While out for a stroll, he had seen a poster announcing Marian's third concert that very evening. He decided to hear this unknown (to him) American contralto.

Marian was drinking a cup of tea with honey in her room backstage during intermission when Mr. Horowitz walked in with Mr. Hurok. After introductions, Mr. Hurok casually asked Marian if she could meet with him the next day. Marian replied casually that she could. But when the door closed behind Mr. Hurok, Marian collapsed in her chair.

How was she ever going to get through the rest of the program without soaring through the roof from excitement? How would she last until morning? All night Marian tossed and turned in her bed. Sol Hurok managed the world's greatest artists, and he had asked to see *her!*

Marian took great care with her appearance, because, she said, people look at her for hours and the sight must be pleasant.

Finally morning came, and Marian went to meet Mr. Hurok. Marian's hands were shaking. She hoped her voice was not. Mr. Hurok asked Marian about her current agency, the number of programs she sang in a year, and the fee she received. His questions went on and on. Then he said the words she had been hoping to hear. "I might be able to do something for you," he said. "I want to present you in your own country."

Before Marian could accept Mr. Hurok's offer, she had to complete a long concert schedule in Europe. By summer's end, she had performed in Russia and in the great European cities of Brussels, Vienna, and Salzburg.

Arturo Toscanini

In Salzburg, Austria, that August, the great Arturo Toscanini came to hear Marian's concert. Toscanini, then the conductor of the New York Philharmonic Orchestra, was world-famous for setting the standards by which classical music was performed. The organizers of the concert saw him in the audience and told Marian he was there just before she walked out on the stage. She felt trembly inside as she bowed to the audience, but her rich voice was firm and confident.

Toscanini came backstage during intermission. When she met the great conductor, Marian's mind went blank. In the minutes before she returned to the stage, she managed to thank him, but she wasn't calm enough to understand exactly what he said.

As always, Marian ended her program with spirituals. Her voice was full of grief and devotion as she sang, "They crucified my Lord, and he never said a mumblin' word." When the last note of "The Crucifixion" vibrated through the concert hall, the audience sat in stunned silence. Kosti's hands trembled with emotion as he closed his music. Then a large sigh rose from the audience, and applause poured over Marian.

After the program, people who had been with Marian during intermission told her Toscanini's exact words. "Yours is a voice," he had said, "such as one hears once in a hundred years."

# 7

# Triumph

As the winter of 1935–1936 approached, Marian got ready to return home. She looked forward to proving herself in her own country, and she could hardly wait to see her family (and Orpheus Fisher) again. It had been a long, successful two years.

Although she knew of other black American performers who had chosen to make their homes in Europe, Marian did not consider it for herself. She could understand very easily why an African American would choose to live in Europe. There she had been treated as a person like everybody else. She had not been turned away from hotels or restaurants or put into filthy train cars because of the color of her skin. It was freedom. It was a burden lifted. But Marian was an American, America was her home, and to America she would return.

There was one terribly difficult decision to make concerning her accompanist. Kosti Vehanen had gone with her all over Scandinavia and Europe. He had helped Marian greatly with her program and languages. He had become a good and faithful friend. Billy King had been her accompanist in the United States and had also been her good and faithful friend. Now Marian had to make a choice.

Having a white accompanist had been taken for granted in Europe, but Marian knew it would be offensive to some (both blacks and whites) in the United States. Her own mother thought she should have a black accompanist.

Marian dreaded hurting Billy's feelings by changing accompanists. But after pacing the floor many nights and debating the problem while she folded and packed her dresses, Marian realized that her accompanist must be the most qualified and most experienced musician. Therefore, she asked Kosti to continue with her. Kosti not only agreed, he had been worried that she would not ask him. "Marian," he said, "if I can come and play only the first pieces on the program, I will charm them so that they will want me to stay."

In September Mr. Hurok told Marian that her first concert after her return was set for December 30, 1935, at New York's Town Hall. Marian shivered a little, remembering again the disaster of her first and only appearance there twelve years before.

Marian and Kosti began preparing for the Town Hall concert immediately. In between their final European concerts, they spent every moment searching for and rehearsing the best possible songs. Kosti was experienced in arranging the proper balance of songs: those to begin with, end with, put in the middle, and the "knockouts" that would make a stunning impression on the audience. By the time they sailed, on December 17, the program was ready. All was going well.

Marian and Kosti on board the *Ile de France* in 1935

Then, on a day when the ocean was heaving and tossing, Marian started to run down the stairs to her cabin for some music. A huge wave slammed into the ship, and Marian slipped and fell with her left foot twisted underneath her. At the bottom of the stairs, Marian slowly unbent her foot, stood up, and held on to the wall. Would she be able to go ahead with her concert? Well, she thought, why not?

The ship's doctor bandaged her foot tightly and told her to stay off it until she saw a doctor at home. She followed his orders until the day of her arrival in New York. Marian laid out the outfit she had planned to wear when she saw her friends and family (and Orpheus Fisher) for the first time in two years. She tried walking on her left foot, without the bandage, and found that it didn't hurt *too* badly. She decided that she could, after all, wear the elegant brown shoes she had bought in Sweden especially for this day.

The arrival was everything she had hoped, and Marian was so excited and overjoyed that she hardly felt the pain in her left ankle. But by the next morning, the day before Christmas, Marian was in the hospital. The doctor showed Marian a broken ankle bone on the X ray, plastered her ankle in a cast that went all the way to her knee, and sent her home to walk on crutches for six weeks.

The evening of the concert, one week later, Marian put on a long black and gold dress that completely covered her cast. At the concert hall, the manager asked if he could make an announcement to the audience about her broken ankle. Absolutely not, Marian said. She did not want an excuse for any part of her performance. Marian was absolutely determined that *this* concert at New York's Town Hall would be a stunning success, with nothing but her singing affecting the audience.

Usually Marian walked proudly to center stage after the curtains opened. This time when the curtains opened, Marian was already standing beside the curve of the piano, her cast hidden by her floor-length dress. Marian's ankle hurt, but pain was far from her thoughts. As she looked out onto the audience, which included America's top music critics, she wondered what they would think of her performance.

Then Kosti, elegant in formal white tie and black tailcoat, struck the first chord. Marian closed her eyes and took a slow, deep breath.

She had chosen to begin the program with "Begrüssung," a song of greeting by George Frideric Handel. This song had such a difficult beginning that it was rarely ever sung in a concert. Marian had to hold the first note for thirty seconds, gradually and steadily increasing the volume without the slightest wavering. She had to be very calm to sustain this long note and make a strong impression on the audience. With all the poise she possessed, Marian sang a perfect first note.

As Marian finished the song, she knew the audience was with her. By the time intermission came, she felt the audience responding to every phrase, and she sang with pure joy uplifting her. Finally, in "The Crucifixion," Marian's rich, vibrant tones soared over the rows of faces glistening with tears.

Marian bowed again and again in response to the audience's ovation, and only when the curtains were finally closed did she remember her broken bone. Perhaps she was thankful for the heavy cast, which kept her from floating away with happiness. At last, Marian could really believe she had made a successful and new beginning in America.

The critics agreed. Howard Taubman of the *New York Times* opened his review by writing, "Let it be said at the outset: Marian Anderson has returned to her native land one of the great singers of our time." Taubman continued by describing her voice as "music-making that proved too deep for words....The very sound of her voice was electrifying. Full, opulent, velvety, it swelled out like a mighty organ."

"One of the greatest singers of our time." —N. Y. TIMES

## MARIAN ANDERSON

"acclaimed greatest concert singer of today"

"holds audience in spell"

"sings way into city's heart"

"leaves lasting impression"

"hailed by huge audience at thrilling concert"

"wild ovation attests to singer's artistry"

"scores brilliant triumph"

—HEADLINES IN AMERICA'S PRESS

As this concert advertisement from the mid-1930s shows, Marian always stood proudly. Her mother told her, "Remember, when you go out on the stage, you've already made an impression before you've even opened your mouth to sing a note."

Marian read the reviews at home sitting by the fire-
place, with her cast covered in a gray woolen sock. The
reviews were quite positive and flattering, she thought,
but as the days passed and the excitement abated, she
took out her music. She examined each song to see
where and how she could improve her performance even
more. Marian knew that now she had reached a higher
level in her career, and she would be compared to the
best concert artists.

After several successful programs in the spring of 1936
in the United States, Marian returned to Europe. She
sang in London, Paris, Vienna, Budapest, Moscow, and
other great cities. At the Paris Opera, where only the
Russian pianist Sergei Rachmaninoff and violinist Fritz
Kreisler had ever given sold-out performances, Marian
Anderson gave a sold-out performance. That night she
wore a stunning gown of gold lamé with a diamond
brooch. As she looked at herself in the mirror, Marian
could hardly believe she was the same woman who a few
years before had thought her career was over. And when
she walked out onstage that night, she smiled at the awe
and pride in Kosti's eyes.

# Easter Sunday

In Europe and at home, Marian Anderson was a success. Over the next few years, she performed in most of Europe's capital cities. Now, in 1939, it was time for her to sing in her own nation's capital.

Washington, D.C., was a segregated, southern city with a large African-American population. The racial lines were firmly, but strangely, drawn. A black artist could perform at the National Theater, for example, but no blacks could be in the audience. Most movie theaters did not admit blacks at all, and one that did had a cement wall down the center, to ensure that blacks were separated from whites. It was in Washington years before that Marian had had to change to a dirty Jim Crow train car.

Marian knew that, at the request of Howard University, Sol Hurok was making arrangements for her appearance at Washington's famous Constitution Hall. He asked for April 9, 1939, but was told that date was already taken. He requested several other dates at the hall for Marian and was surprised to learn that every date was already taken. Puzzled, he asked another concert manager to request the same dates for another performer, who happened to be white. Every date was available.

Marian and Sol were shocked. Her voice, her reputation, her honors, her world renown did not matter. All that mattered was the color of her skin, and according to the Washington chapter of the Daughters of the American Revolution (DAR), who owned Constitution Hall, Marian Anderson's skin was the wrong color. The DAR refused to allow a black artist to appear at the hall.

Marian did not fight back. She went right on with her other concerts and kept the hurt of this insult to herself as she always did. And she thought of what her mother said: "Do the best you can, and the Lord will do what you can not."

In February 1939, Marian sang in San Francisco. On her way to the concert hall, she passed a newsstand, glanced at the daily paper, and gasped.

"MRS. ROOSEVELT TAKES STAND:

RESIGNS FROM D.A.R.,"

shouted the headline. Eleanor Roosevelt, the wife of the president of the United States, had resigned from the DAR because of Marian Anderson. Marian had met Mrs. Roosevelt in 1936, when she gave a private concert at the White House, and she admired Mrs. Roosevelt greatly. Now she admired Mrs. Roosevelt even more, for this was a bold public stand against discrimination—certain to make some Americans very angry.

And it did. People all over the country began to talk about Marian Anderson and the DAR. As much as Marian wanted to keep the shame of such treatment to herself, it was now out in the open in front of the whole world.

**CONSTITUTION HALL**

Washington, D. C.

THIS AGREEMENT, Made this Twentieth day of August 19 35, between the National Society, Daughters of the American Revolution, a body corporate, duly incorporated and existing under the laws of the United States as a society organized wholly for educational, historical and patriotic purposes and

at no time for profit (hereinafter called the Lessor) and THE PHILADELPHIA ORCHESTRA (hereinafter called the Lessee).

WITNESSETH: That the Lessor does hereby let, demise and lease to the Lessee and the Lessee does hereby hire and take from the Lessor, the use of the CONSTITUTION HALL, situated in Washington, D.C., together with the stage and the corridors, foyers and vestibules leading thereto (except the pipe organ for which a nominal additional charge is made) for a term of 4 hours, commencing at 7 P.M. o'clock, on October 24th, 1935, December 19th, 1935, March 12th, 1936 and April 2nd, 1936

the said premises to be used by the Lessee for the purpose of CONCERT BY WHITE ARTISTS ONLY

and for no other purpose or purposes at a total rental of Sixteen Hundred Dollars ($400.00) ($1,600.00), of which Four Hundred Dollars/ have been paid at the time of signing hereof and the balance of Three Hundred Dollars ($300.00) for each concert to be paid on or before noon on October 24th, 1935, December 19th, 1935, March 12th, 1936 and April 2nd, 1936.

This lease is made upon the foregoing and following terms agreements and conditions, all and everyone of which the parties hereto agree to observe,

In this agreement with the Philadelphia Orchestra to rent Constitution Hall in 1935, the Daughters of the American Revolution (DAR) stipulate, "CONCERT BY WHITE ARTISTS ONLY."

At night, when she couldn't sleep, Marian tried to sort out her feelings. She felt sad. She felt ashamed as an American. She felt "sorry for the people who had precipitated the affair." And, she had to admit, she felt bitter, for she was as entitled to sing in Constitution Hall as any other artist. It seemed impossible to Marian that, because she was black, people in her own country would prevent her from singing in a fine hall in her own nation's capital.

The controversy raised emotions and tempers that seemed to increase daily. The problem would not go away, and Americans were taking sides noisily. Neighbors argued, students debated, and white Americans who had never before given racial discrimination a thought were giving it thought now. Marian and the DAR were discussed on the front pages of the newspapers, in the editorials, on the radio, and over the back fence.

The ladies of the DAR did not change their minds. They did not apologize. But the controversy was resolved. Officials of the Department of the Interior invited Marian to sing in Washington at the Lincoln Memorial, the nation's symbol of freedom for all.

It was the perfect place. Abraham Lincoln, the sixteenth president of the United States, wrote the Emancipation Proclamation, a document which freed the slaves in the Confederate states during the Civil War. And carved into the marble of the memorial were President Lincoln's words describing the United States: "...a new nation, conceived in liberty and dedicated to the proposition that all men are created equal."

The concert was to take place on Easter Sunday, April 9, 1939. Marian had other concerts to perform in the meantime, and at every single one reporters asked, "What about Washington?" And with every passing day, Marian found it harder to explain her feelings.

Early in the morning on Easter Sunday, Marian and her mother arrived in Washington. (They stayed in a private home, because hotels would not admit them.) Then Marian and Kosti drove to the Lincoln Memorial to look over the preparations. Six microphones would broadcast her concert not only to the people present but also to a radio audience from Maine to California. Marian began to feel shivery inside as she looked over the vast open expanse that spread before the memorial.

When Marian returned that afternoon, policemen formed an aisle for her to pass through. She was vaguely aware that it was a glorious day, with the sun shining through clouds onto the brilliant cherry blossoms and soft green grass of spring. Over the noise of her heart, she heard the voices of an enormous multitude. When she finally stepped out in front of the great seated statue of Abraham Lincoln, she was almost overwhelmed by what she saw. There, with uplifted faces, was a throng that stretched all the way from the foot of the Lincoln Memorial to the Washington Monument.

Marian tried to swallow. She tried to catch her breath. She knew there were people on the platform with her, people introducing her, saying things about her, but she did not hear them. Kosti struck the first chords of "America," and it was time for Marian to sing.

Marian, with Kosti at the piano, performed for 75,000 people at the Easter Sunday concert. Millions of listeners across America heard her on the radio.

For a desperate moment, Marian could not remember a word. Then the words and the breath and the music came to her. "My country 'tis of thee," she sang, "Sweet land of liberty." Some in the audience wept as Marian sang of freedom. She felt as if she were not there at all, but was watching from afar. She felt the great waves of emotion coming from the people and heard the great roar of applause.

When the concert was finished, Marian could not remember one song she had sung or one word she had said. Fortunately, all the music and all the words were written down. The next day, when she felt calmer, Marian read the report in the newspaper. She read the names of the people who were there, what they said, what she said, and what she wore.

Marian read the introduction that Harold Ickes, Secretary of the Interior, gave her. "Genius, like justice, is blind," Mr. Ickes had said. "Genius draws no color line."

Marian read that other members of the cabinet, justices of the Supreme Court, representatives, senators, and her mother were there on the platform with her. She read that she sang "America," "O mio Fernando," Schubert's "Ave Maria," and the spirituals "My Soul Is Anchored in the Lord," "Gospel Train," and "Trampin'." She read that the audience would not stop applauding and calling for her until she returned to the microphone.

Marian and Harold Ickes standing before the Lincoln Memorial, Easter Sunday 1939

"I am overwhelmed," Marian had said to the crowd, "I just can't talk. I can't tell you what you have done for me today. I thank you from the bottom of my heart again and again." There it was in the newspaper, but Marian could not remember saying a word of it.

DAR members with their narrow wisdom, said Kosti, had closed the door to an indoor hall. But, Kosti wrote, "God in His great wisdom opened the door to His most beautiful cathedral...that glorious Easter Sunday."

# 9

# Everyday Discrimination

After her Easter Sunday concert, Marian could begin to believe that the success she had once only dared hope for was really hers. In June 1939, she sang at the White House for the second time, in a special concert for the king and queen of England. The next month, Mrs. Roosevelt presented Marian with the Spingarn Medal. This honor is awarded by the National Association for the Advancement of Colored People (NAACP) to the black American who has attained the noblest achievement in any honorable pursuit.

At the end of the 1939–1940 season, during which Marian gave ninety-two concerts, Kosti Vehanen had to return to Finland because of poor health. Marian wanted what was best for him, but she would miss him terribly. Kosti had been her accompanist, adviser, and friend since her career first began its rise to success.

Franz Rupp became Marian's accompanist in 1940.

Marian's new accompanist, Franz Rupp, was just as skilled and likable as Kosti. Franz, who had traveled with other well-known vocalists, knew that reviewers considered Marian "the world's greatest contralto." So he was all the more shocked when he saw how she was treated in her own country.

One evening in Birmingham, Alabama, Marian and Franz looked for a pleasant restaurant where they could eat before their concert. In all of Birmingham, they couldn't find a restaurant that would serve dinner to the world's greatest contralto. A restaurant in the train station agreed to serve her a sandwich—but only outside.

Marian had no explanation for Franz. For her it was not new or shocking. She had toured the Jim Crow south often enough to know that this was an ordinary and everyday experience for many black Americans. Marian's Easter Sunday concert was over. Discrimination was not.

White-only diners, like this one in Ohio, were common when Marian toured in the United States in the 1940s.

As Marian's schedule grew, Mr. Hurok sent her a personal manager, Isaac Alexander Jofe. Jofe planned the itinerary and the free days between concerts. He watched the train schedule, got the taxis, counted the luggage, and paid the bills. He made sure the piano was in the right place on the stage, the lights were ready, and the dressing room was prepared. He also made sure hot tea with honey was waiting for Marian at intermission, and that there was a supper of sandwiches after the concert.

Marian knew that even Jofe sometimes had difficulty finding a hotel room for her, but she tried to keep it out of her mind. "It is more comfortable not to think about it if I can avoid it...," she said, sadly. "If my mind dwells even partly on the disconcerting thought that I am staying where I am not really welcome, I cannot go out and sing as though my heart were full of love and happiness."

A Birmingham, Alabama, bus with Jim Crow signs

While traveling around the United States, Marian usually cooked and ate her meals in her hotel room. She insisted that she really wanted to do this. Actually, Marian had been told by various hotel managers that she was certainly welcome to eat in the hotel dining room, but "other guests might complain."

Still Marian kept her gracious manner. She believed that if white people could see that they were wrong about her, they might see that they were wrong about black people in general. Sometimes she felt successful. Sometimes a hotel manager who was cold to her when she arrived said, "We were glad to have you. Please come again," when she left. But sometimes the circumstances of Marian's life were so peculiar that she would have laughed, had she not been so hurt.

There was the time in Atlantic City, New Jersey, when she was honored with the keys to the city—and refused a room in a hotel. There was the time in Springfield, Illinois, when she sang at the opening of a film on Abraham Lincoln—and was refused a room in the Lincoln Hotel. There was the time she sang in Kalamazoo, Michigan, and was allowed to stay in a hotel—as long as she went up to her room in the freight elevator.

When Marian faced discrimination in hotels and other places, it hurt her. But what hurt even more was knowing that African Americans were turned away from some of her concerts or were forced to sit apart from whites, often in the worst seats. Finally Marian decided that she would no longer sing in segregated halls. Some halls changed their rules when Marian made her position clear, but some did not, and to those she would not go. She was sorry, she said, but she was standing on principle.

# 10

# Dreams to Fulfill

Marian Anderson finally married her high school sweetheart, Orpheus ("King") Fisher, in July 1943. They married after much hesitation and several European tours on her part and twenty years of patient waiting on his part. It was worth the wait, they agreed.

Their first house, a farmhouse, was a big, old-fashioned place, but both Marian and King dreamed of a home with all the modern conveniences. Before the dream house came along, they looked at many "properties that were not available to us," Marian said, tactfully. (White owners would not sell to them.) Then they found the perfect location in Connecticut. King, an architect, designed and helped build their home, which they named Marianna Farm. Marianna Farm had everything they wanted, from an up-to-date kitchen to horses, cows, two very large pigs, chickens, dogs, cats, a pond, and apple trees. Best of all, King built a separate music studio where Marian and Franz could practice as long and as loudly as they wanted.

*Above:* Marian at Marianna Farm

*Right:* Marian and King leaving a concert hall. Because of his light skin color, King was more successful shopping for land in Connecticut when he went by himself.

It must have seemed to Marian's friends and family that now she had all her heart desired. And she did, but for one dream still unfulfilled.

When she was a child, Marian had dreamed of being in the Metropolitan Opera in New York City. When she was a teenager, she had saved her money and bought tickets when the Metropolitan appeared in Philadelphia. How wonderful it would be to sing in an opera, she had thought—until she learned that black singers were not welcome. Her dream of singing in an opera would remain just a dream.

Then one day in September 1954, Sol Hurok invited Marian and her husband to a performance at the Metropolitan Opera in New York and to a grand opening reception afterwards. At the reception, Rudolf Bing, the tall and lanky general manager of the Metropolitan Opera, walked over to Marian. He came straight to the point.

"Would you be interested in singing with the Metropolitan?" he asked.

Marian stared at him. She wasn't quite sure he was serious. He repeated the offer.

"I think I would," she said.

Mr. Bing told Marian they were considering her for the part of Ulrica, in Giuseppe Verdi's opera *The Masked Ball (Un Ballo in Maschera)*. He asked if she knew the part. She didn't. In fact, Marian didn't know any part in any opera, but she eagerly made plans to learn this one.

A few days later, Mr. Hurok called with one word: "Congratulations!"

Marian Anderson and Rudolf Bing on the stage of the Metropolitan Opera House in October 1954

It had been decided; Marian Anderson would perform with the Metropolitan Opera. Marian was so excited she phoned her mother and stammered out the news. Then she called her husband, and then she called Franz Rupp.

Now she really had to go to work, and it wasn't just singing. The role of Ulrica was small, but vital to the story. Ulrica, a Gypsy fortune-teller, dramatically tells the hero of the opera that he will die "at the hand of a friend." Marian had to learn to act the part of a vibrant and vivid Gypsy, while singing, and while all the people around her were acting and singing, too. She not only sang her own solo part, but also sang in duets, trios, and with the entire chorus, all in Italian. Marian loved the excitement of orchestra, singers, costumes, staging, and every tiny detail joining together to form an opera.

January 7, 1955, was opening night. Marian was backstage early for makeup, costume, and voice warm-up. Jofe was there, fussing over everything.

Out in the hall, Marian's family and Mr. Hurok were already seated in the center box (the box saved for kings, queens, and presidents). The audience was gradually filling every seat. In the lobby, news photographers scrambled to take pictures of some of the very distinguished guests: Ralph Bunche, Langston Hughes, the Duchess of Windsor, and Helen Keller (who could only *feel* Marian's music).

Marian had always been rather proud of the fact that she was not nervous before a peformance. But when the curtain rose for scene two, revealing Marian alone on the stage of the Metropolitan Opera, she trembled. She calmed herself and sang, but she knew her voice was not coming out smoothly, and there was nothing she could do about it. Her throat was tight with emotion. Just as on Easter Sunday 1939, Marian was more than a woman with a beautiful voice. She was a symbol for all African Americans.

At the end of the act, the audience responded with an amazing eight curtain calls. Backstage, her mother hugged her and whispered, "We thank the Lord." That was enough for Marian.

When the season was over, Marian was asked to perform the same role the next year, and she accepted with gladness. Singing with the Metropolitan Opera was, she said, the greatest pleasure of her entire musical career, for "then I knew I had not dreamed the impossible dream."

Marian takes a curtain call (right) and is congratulated by her mother (above) after her debut performance with the Metropolitan Opera.

# Legacy

Marian Anderson's Easter Sunday concert in 1939 was one of the great civil rights events of the twentieth century. There at the Lincoln Memorial, people saw and heard an African-American woman with an extraordinary voice. She stood before the nation as a symbol of what all black Americans could do.

In 1955 Marian Anderson again made history when she became the first black singer to appear with the Metropolitan Opera. Her performance ended forever racial segregation in opera and opened the gates for great black singers such as Jessye Norman, Leontyne Price, Kathleen Battle, and many more.

In 1957 Marian toured the Far East as a goodwill ambassador for the State Department, and in 1958 President Dwight Eisenhower appointed her a delegate to the United Nations. In 1963 she received the Presidential Medal of Freedom, the highest civilian honor that can be given to an American citizen.

Marian Anderson, United States delegate to the United Nations, in 1958

Marian Anderson sang for kings, queens, and presidents all over the world. She received countless tributes and honors. But greater than any honor she received is the gift she gave to Americans. She gave us the gift of dignity, the opportunity to correct wrongs, and the moral courage to break down the walls that separate whites and blacks in America. "As a nation," said Leontyne Price, "we owe her gratitude for showing that talent and dignity can prevail."

Marian raised her voice not in anger, but in song. She never made a public statement against racism, but she worked to turn minds away from prejudice every time she walked onto a stage.

For African-American singers, Marian Anderson was a role model. She made the path. "Because of you, I am," said one singer.

For all African Americans, Marian Anderson's example of persistence, unfailing courtesy, and undaunted spirit has been an inspiration to achieve goals that otherwise might have seemed out of reach.

For all people, Marian Anderson represented what, in Jessye Norman's words, "is wonderful, simple, pure and majestic in the human spirit." She was the essence of grace. One did not have to be black or American or even a music lover, wrote the editor of *Opera News,* to be touched by Marian Anderson in a way that words cannot describe. "One only had to be human."

Marian Anderson died on April 8, 1993. Her legacy continues. "I wasn't a great fighter," Marian said. "I hope that my work will speak."

And it has.

## "What I had was singing."

Marian Anderson (1897–1993)

# Notes

page 7

Webster's dictionary says discrimination is "the practice of treating persons or things in different ways because of prejudice." This is what Marian Anderson experienced.

page 10

Marian's birth certificate was found after her death. Before this, all sources (and Marian herself) gave 1902 as her birth year. Because of this new information, many events in her life before 1921 are now difficult to date reliably. Marian's reasons for the birth date discrepancy remain a mystery.

page 25

The Philadelphia music school that rejected Marian no longer exists.

page 27

Marian probably studied with Mr. Boghetti for five or six years.

page 28

Spirituals "are my own music," Marian said. Traditionally, spirituals express a slave's yearning for liberation, even if the freedom exists only in the imagination.

page 38

Even after her long and successful career, Marian said that the best moment of her entire life was when she told her mother she didn't have to work anymore.

Marian and Franz worked on hundreds of songs each year. It took months to choose just the right ones for Marian's many long programs.

page 64

Music critics and reviewers, from the *New York Times* to the smallest local newspaper, tried to describe Marian's voice. They said it was "rich and full, clear as crystal, mellow as autumn," "great, gorgeous," "brilliant, tender, effortless, magical, stunning...," and "one of the world's most beautiful voices."

The great American soprano Jessye Norman first heard Marian Anderson's voice on a recording and said, "I could not believe this was a human voice." And a woman in Los Angeles remarked, "Her tone was so vibrant I could almost touch it. It was like rum-raisin ice cream."

page 79

Marian's regal dignity and ability caused white-owned southern newspapers to alter their traditional treatment of nonwhites. For the first time, a black woman was referred to as physically attractive. Marian was called "slender, charming" and a "tall brown goddess." Southern newspapers praised her voice, her dignified beauty, and her elegant dresses. They didn't go so far as to call her "Miss Anderson," however, for at that time southern papers did not give black Americans the honor of a title. Instead, the papers spoke of "Singer Anderson."

# Bibliography

## Books:

Anderson, Marian. *My Lord, What a Morning.* New York: Viking Press, 1956.

Hurok, Sol and Ruth Goode. *Impresario: A Memoir.* New York: Random House, 1946.

Newman, Shirlee P. *Marian Anderson: Lady from Philadelphia.* Philadelphia: Westminster Press, 1966.

*Patterson, Charles. *Marian Anderson.* New York: Franklin Watts, 1988.

Rupp, Franz, editor. *Marian Anderson: Album of Songs and Spirituals.* New York: G. Schirmer, 1948.

Sims, Janet L. *Marian Anderson: An Annotated Bibliography and Discography.* Westport, CT: Greenwood Press, 1981.

*Tedards, Anne. *Marian Anderson.* New York: Chelsea House Publishers, 1988.

Vehanen, Kosti. *Marian Anderson: A Portrait.* New York: Whittlesey House, 1941.

## Articles:

Anderson, Marian. "Some Reflections on Singing," as told to Rose Heylbut. *Etude* 57 (October 1939).

Blau, Eleanor. "Marian Anderson, 50 Years After Rebuff." *International Herald Tribune* (August 16, 1989).

Burroughs, Bruce. "Marian Anderson: A Voice for the Ages." *Los Angeles Times* (April 10, 1993).

DePreist, James. "Grounded in Faith, Free to Fly." *New York Times* (April 18, 1993).

*A star denotes a book for younger readers.

Eleanor Roosevelt, presenting Marian with the Spingarn Medal in 1939

Di Nardo, Tom. "World Loses Sweet Voice." *Philadelphia Daily News* (April 9, 1993).

Emmons, Shirlee. "Voices from the Past: Marian Anderson." *NATS Journal* 42 (November/December 1985).

Fisher, Isaac. "Marian Anderson." *Southern Workman* 65 (March 1936).

Folkart, Burt A. "Pioneering Singer Marian Anderson Dies." *Los Angeles Times* (April 9, 1993).

Forbes, Elizabeth. "Marian Anderson." *Independent,* London, England (April 9, 1993).

Hawkins, William. "Marian Anderson Says Farewell." *Musical America* 84 (September 1964).

Hayes, Patrick. "White Artists Only." *Washingtonian* 24 (April 1989).

Heilbut, Anthony. "Marian Anderson." *New Yorker* (April 26, 1993).

Honan, William H. "D.A.R. and Marian Anderson: Fresh Perspective on a Rebuff." *New York Times* (May 18, 1993).

Hurok, Sol. "Talent Isn't Enough!" *Etude* 67 (September 1949).

Klaw, Barbara. "A Voice One Hears Once in a Hundred Years." *American Heritage* 28 (February 1977).

Kolodin, Irving. "Marian Anderson Makes History." *Saturday Review* 38 (January 22, 1955).

Kozinn, Allan. "Marian Anderson Is Dead at 96; Singer Shattered Racial Barriers." *New York Times* (April 9, 1993).

Kyuper, George A. "Marian Anderson." *Southern Workman* 61 (March 1932).

Lewis, Claude. "Anderson Used Her Great Voice to Send a Message of Civil Rights." *Philadelphia Inquirer* (April 12, 1993).

"Marian Anderson 1897–1993." *Time* (April 19, 1993).

"Marian Anderson Holds Student Body Spellbound." *Hampton Script* 8 (January 18, 1936).

"Marian Anderson Sings in Musical Art Concert." *Hampton Script* 10 (March 14, 1938).

"Marian Anderson's Aria to America." Editorial. *Sunday Oregonian* (April 11, 1993).

"Reflected Glory." *Opera News* 48 (October 1983).

Stabler, David. "Contralto Marian Anderson Dies at 96." *Oregonian* (April 9, 1993).

Weatherby, W. J. "The Singer Is the Song." *Guardian,* Manchester, England (April 9, 1993).

Webster, Daniel. "The Legendary Singer Marian Anderson Dies." *Philadelphia Inquirer* (April 9, 1993).

## Films:

"The Lady from Philadelphia." Edward R. Murrow, producer. *See It Now.* CBS. December 30, 1957.

*Marian Anderson.* PBS documentary film. Los Angeles, CA, KCET. May 8, 1991.

All quotations in this biography were taken from the above sources.

# Index

Selected quotations from *My Lord, What a Morning* by Marian Anderson. Copyright © 1956, renewed 1984 by Marian Anderson. Used by permission of Viking Penguin, a division of Penguin Books USA Inc.
Illustrations are reproduced through the courtesy of: UPI/Bettmann, front cover; Mitchell Jamieson, *An Incident in Contemporary American Life, 1942.* Interior Department, Washington, D.C., David Allison, photographer, back cover; Schomburg Center for Research in Black Culture, pp. 2, 57, 65; Special Collections, Van Pelt Library, University of Pennsylvania, pp. 6, 19, 28, 33, 37, 49, 54, 62, 73, 76, 81 (both), 83, 85 (bottom), 91; Urban Archives, Temple University, Philadelphia, PA, pp. 8, 21, 85 (top); MG219/Pennsylvania State Archives, pp. 11, 15; Colin P. Varga, pp. 17, 36; Moorland-Spingarn Research Center, p. 22; Florida State Archives, p. 31; Music Division, The New York Public Library, Astor, Lenox, and Tilden Foundation, p. 42; Library of Congress, pp. 50, 72, 77; Independent Picture Service, p. 58; *The Washingtonian,* p. 69; Birmingham Public Library, p. 78; United Nations, p. 87; *Danbury News-Times,* p. 89; National Archives, p. 93.